MW01245169

ASSURED BY ABBA

100 BIBLICAL AFFIRMATIONS

FOR DAILY MOTIVATION

BY SAMAJA M. STEVENSON

This Book Belongs To

_____

Date

_____

Occasion

_____

Copy Rights Page

ASSURED BY ABBA

100 BIBLICAL AFFIRMATIONS
FOR DAILY MOTIVATION

SAMAJA M. STEVENSON

ISBN: 979-8-218-34747-5

Book Author: Samaja M. Stevenson

Published by: She's Favored Network, LLC for Samaja M. Stevenson

Table of Content

To my dearest granny,

Words cannot express the immense love and gratitude I have for you. Throughout my life, you have been my guiding star, always there to offer your wisdom and support. Your unwavering love and kindness have shaped me into the person I am today.

From the countless stories you've shared to the life lessons you've imparted, you have shown me the true meaning of strength and resilience. Your presence in my life has been a constant source of comfort and inspiration.

This book is dedicated to you, my beloved grandmother, as a tribute to the beautiful bond we share. Each page within these covers is a testament to the impact you have had on my life. Your love and guidance have shaped my values, my dreams, and my aspirations.

I am forever grateful for the countless memories we've created together, from the laughter-filled family gatherings to the cooking lessons and conversation. Your unwavering support and belief in me have given me the confidence to pursue my dreams and reach for the stars.

Thank you, Grandma, for your unconditional love, your gentle encouragement, and the countless ways you have enriched my life. You are truly a remarkable woman, and I am blessed to call you my granny.

With all my love and appreciation,
Samaja Stevenson

To my amazing sister,

You are not just my sibling, but also my best friend. Throughout the ups and downs of life, you have always been there for me, offering your unwavering support and love. This book is dedicated to you, as a token of my appreciation.

From childhood adventures to late-night heart-to-heart conversations, we have created many memories that I will cherish forever. You have been my rock, my cheerleader, and my partner in crime.

Thank you for being by my side through thick and thin, for celebrating my successes and comforting me during tough times. Your presence in my life brings me so much joy and happiness. I am grateful for the laughter, the tears, and the unconditional love we have shared.

This book is a tribute to our unbreakable bond, a reminder of the beautiful connection we have as sisters. May it serve as a reminder of the love and gratitude I have for you, today and always.

With all my love,
Your big sister

Hey there, amazing readers!

I wanted to take a moment to express my deepest gratitude for your incredible support. Your belief in me and this affirmation book means the world to me. Throughout this journey, I've poured my heart into crafting each affirmation, with the hope of inspiring and uplifting you. I wanted to create a book that would serve as a guiding light, reminding you of your inner strength and limitless potential through Christ.

Your enthusiasm and encouragement have been the driving force behind this project. Your kind words and messages of appreciation have touched my heart and motivated me to keep pushing forward. I truly believe that together, we can create a positive ripple effect in the world. By embracing the power of biblical affirmations and cultivating a mindset of self-belief, we can overcome any challenge and achieve greatness.

So, thank you from the bottom of my heart for joining me on this incredible journey. Your support has made all the difference. I can't wait for you to dive into the pages of this book and discover the transformative power of biblical affirmations. Remember, you are capable, you are worthy, and you have the power to create a life filled with joy and abundance.

With love and gratitude,

Samaja Stevenson

How to Guide:

1. Create a safe space: Find a comfortable spot where you can relax and focus on the affirmations. It could be a cozy corner in your room or a serene outdoor setting. I recommend starting your day with the affirmations so that you can practice visualizing throughout your day.

2. Set an intention: Before diving into the book, set an intention for your reading session. What do you hope to gain or achieve? Having a clear intention will help you connect with the word of God on a deeper level.

3. Take it slow: Don't rush through the book. Take your time with each affirmation, allowing its message to sink in. Reflect on the words and let them resonate with you.

4. Read out loud: To enhance the impact of the affirmations, try reading them out loud. Speaking the words aloud makes them a declaration and the words become more powerful within your life.

How to Guide Continued:

5. Visualize and feel: As you read each affirmation, try to visualize and feel the positive outcome it describes. Imagine yourself embodying the qualities or experiences mentioned through Christ. This can amplify the effectiveness of the affirmations.

6. Practice daily: Consistency is key! Make it a habit to read from your affirmation book regularly, ideally every day. Repetition and consistent exposure to biblical affirmations can have a profound impact on your mindset and well-being.

Remember, an affirmation book is a tool for self-discovery and personal growth. Embrace the journey and allow the affirmations to uplift and inspire you. Enjoy the process and let the word of God flow!

ASSURED BY ABBA

100 BIBLICAL AFFIRMATIONS

FOR DAILY MOTIVATION

Part 1

I AM

I am a child of the most high God

John 1:12

But to as many as did receive and welcome Him, He gave the right to become children of God, *that is, to those who believe in His name-*

_____

I am not who I once was: I am forgiven

_____

2 Corinthians 5:17

Therefore if anyone is in Christ , he is a *new* creature; the old things have passed away. Behold, new things have come.

I am called to be a light to the world

---

1 Peter 2:9

But you are *A CHOSEN RACE, a royal PRIESTHOOD, A CONSECRATED NATION, A PEOPLE FOR God's OWN POSSESSION,* so that you may proclaim the excellencies of Him who called you out of darkness into His marvelous light.

I am designed for greatness

Ephesians 2:10

For we are His workmanship, created in Christ Jesus for good works, which God prepared beforehand , so that we would walk in them.

I am made to be exceptional

Psalms 119:73

Your hands have made me and established me; Give me understanding and a teachable heart, that I may learn Your commandments.

I am blessed coming in and going out

Deuteronomy 28:6

"You will be blessed when you come in and you will be blessed when you go out".

I am loved

John 3:16

"For God so loved and dearly prized the world, that He gave His only begotten Son, and whoever believes and trust in Him shall not perish, but have eternal life.

———————————

I am wonderful

———————————

Psalms 138:14

I will give thanks and praise to You, for I am fearfully and wonderfully made; Wonderful are Your works, And my soul knows it very well.

———————

I am adopted

———————

Assured by Abba

Romans 8:15

For you have not
received a spirit of
adoption as sons by
which we cry, "Abba!
Father!"

emotions severely hamper your life, and now is the moment to deal with them.

"Forgiveness is to give up resentment," as defined by Merriam-Webster. It continues in some kind. "to stop holding a grudge against a wrongdoer." Reread that. To "stop holding a grudge against a wrongdoer." All that is happening is that you are letting out some pent-up anger and an audible "Ohh!" Every time you dwell on it, it will suffocate and harm you.

To let go of the anger is a more accurate description of your actions.

Here is an example of letting go of anger as a means of forgiving. Many years ago, Doris Roberts son's walked into an Amish school and killed all the children there. The Amish community approached Doris the night of the shooting and offered her and her family forgiveness. After this, she spent the last 10 to 15 years as part of that community, being a family, and being a mother to the one girl who did not die but will be immobilized for the rest of her life. That's the most profound level of mercy. For although she did not personally cause the deaths, she carried the guilt for her son's actions, and it was only after the Amish forgave her and accepted her into their community that she could move on with her life and help others. Thus, I urge you to give this idea some consideration.

How Do You Forgive?

Forgiving someone means giving up any chance of a better past, which can be difficult because it brings up painful emotions like anger and sadness. Past mistakes are irrevocable. It is a method for

I am chosen

1 Peter 2:9

But you are *A CHOSEN RACE, a royal PRIESTHOOD, A CONSECRATED NATION, A PEOPLE FOR God's OWN POSSESSION,* so that you may proclaim the excellencies of Him who called you out of darkness into His marvelous light.

I am safe

---

2 Timothy 4:18

The Lord will rescue me from every evil assault, and He will bring me safely into His heavenly kingdom; to Him be the glory forever and ever. Amen.

I am holy

---

1 Peter 1:16

because it is written,
"*YOU SHALL BE
HOLY, FOR I AM
HOLY*".

I am not alone

Deuteronomy 31:6

"Be strong and courageous, do not be afraid or tremble in dread before them, for it is the LORD your God who goes with you. He will not fail you or abandon you,"

I am anxious for nothing, but in everything, by prayer and supplication, with thanks, I present my request to God

---

Philippians 4:6

"Be strong and courageous, do not be afraid or tremble in dread before them, for it is the LORD your God who goes with you. He will not fail you or abandon you,"

I am saved

Ephesians 2:8

For it is by grace that you have been saved through faith. And this is not of yourselves, but it is the gift of God;

_____

I am secure

_____

John 10:28

"And I give them eternal life, and they will never, ever perish; and no one will ever snatch them out of My hand."

Assured by Abba

_____

I am strong

_____

2 Corinthians 12:10

So I am well pleased with weakness, with insults, with distresses, with persecutions, and with difficulties, for the sake of Christ; for when I am weak, then I am strong.

I am not timid

---

2 Timothy 1:7

For God did not give us a spirit of timidity or cowardice or fear, but of power and of love and of sound judgement and personal discipline.

I am heard

---

1 John 5:14

This is the confidence which we have before Him: that if we ask anything according to His will, He hears us.

I am healed

Isaiah 53:5

But He was wounded for our transgressions, He was crushed for our wickedness; The punishment for our wellbeing fell on Him, And by His stripes we are healed.

———————————

I am delivered

———————————

Psalms 34:4

I sought the LORD,
and He answered me,
And delivered me
from all my fears.

I am accepted

Romans 15:7

Therefore, accept and welcome one another, just as Christ has accepted and welcomed us to the glory of God.

I am comforted

John 14:26

But the Helper, the Holy Spirit, whom the Father will send in My name, He will teach you all things. And He will help you remember everything that I have told you.

I am protected

Psalms 3:3

But You, O LORD, are a shield for me, My glory, and the One who lifts my head.

I am forgiven

---

1 John 1:9

If we admit that we have sinned and confess our sins, He is faithful and just, and will forgive our sins and cleanse us continually from all unrighteousness.

I am justified

Romans 5:1

THEREFORE, SINCE we have been justified by faith, through our Lord Jesus Christ.

I am set apart

Romans 12:2

And do not be conformed to this world, but be transformed and progressively changed, so that you may prove what the will of God is, that which is good and acceptable and perfect.

———————

I am sanctified

———————

1 Thessalonians 5:23

Now may the God of peace Himself sanctify you through and through; and may your spirit and soul and body be kept complete and blameless at the coming of our Lord Jesus Chrsit.

I am made new

---

2 Corinthians 5:17

Therefore if anyone is in Christ , he is a new creature; the old things have passed away. Behold, new things have come.

I am approved

---

2 Timothy 2:15

Study and do your best to present yourself to God approved, a workman who has no reason to be ashamed, accurately handling and skillfully teaching the word of truth.

I am redeemed

Ephesians 1:7

In Him we have redemption through His blood, the forgiveness and complete pardon of our sin, in accordance with the riches of His grace

---

I am renewed

Colossians 3:10

and have put on the new self who is being continually renewed in true knowledge in the image of Him who created the new self-

---

I am victorious

Romans 8:37

Yet in all these things we are more than conquerors and gain an overwhelming victory through Him who loved us.

I am seen

Psalms 33:18

Behold, the eye of
the LORD is upon
those who fear Him,
On those who hope in
His compassion and
lovingkindness,

I am equipped

2 Timothy 3:17

so that the man of
God may be complete
and proficient,
outfitted and
throughly equipped
for every good work.

I am set free

John 8:36

So if the Son makes you free, then you are unquestionably free.

I am more than a conqueror. I will overcome

Romans 8:37

Yet in all these things we are more than conquerors and gain an overwhelming victory through Him who loved us.

I am God's precious
child, and he will
never forget me. My
name is written on
his hand

Isaiah 49:15-16

...Even these may forget, but I will not forget you. Indeed, I have inscribed you on the palms of my hands;...

I am fearfully and wonderfully made

Psalms 139:14

I will give thanks and praise to You, for I am fearfully and wonderfully made; Wonderful are Your works, And my soul knows it very well.

_____

I am special

_____

Ephesians 2:10

For we are His workmanship, created in Christ Jesus for good works, which God prepared beforehand , so that we would walk in them.

I am intelligent

Genesis 1:27

So God created man in His own image, in the image and likeness of God He created him; male and female He created them.

I am brave

Romans 8:28

And we know that God causes all things to work together for good for those who love God, to those who are called according to His plan and purpose.

I am free from the chains of guilt, shame, and condemnation

Romans 8:1

THEREFORE THERE is now no condemnation for those who are in Christ Jesus.

I am not afraid for God has not given me the spirit of fear

---

2 Timothy 1:7

For God did not give us a spirit of timidity or cowardice or fear, but of power and of love and of sound judgement and personal discipline.

I am filled with power

Micah 3:8

But in fact, I am filled with power, With the Spirit of the Lord, And with justice and might,...

I am diligent and faithful in my works. I will experience success and increase

---

Proverbs 22:29

Do you see a man skillful and experienced in his work? He will stand before kings; He will not stand before obscure men.

I am a blessing to others, and through me, God's favor flows abundantly

---

Genesis 12:2

...And I will bless you abundantly, And make your name great, And you shall be a blessing;

I am God's workmanship, created in Christ for good works

Ephesians 2:10

For we are His workmanship, created in Christ Jesus for good works, which God prepared beforehand , so that we would walk in them.

Part 2

Declarations

No weapon formed against me shall prosper

Isaiah 54:17

"No weapon that is formed against you will succeed; every tongue that rises against you in judgement you will condemn. This is. the heritage of the servants of the Lord, And this is their vindication from Me," says the LORD.

Assured by Abba

I extend love

Galatians 5:22-23

But the fruits of the Spirit is love, joy, peace, patience, kindness, goodness, fruitfulness, gentleness, self-control. Against such things there is no law.

I have everything
I need to flourish

---

2 Peter 1:3

For His divine power has
bestowed on us
everything necessary
for life and godliness,
through true and
personal knowledge of
Him who called us by His
glory and excellence.

Jesus said "it is finished", so I will stop trying to prove myself by my own works

---

John 19:30

...He said, "It's finished!'
And He bowed His
head and gave up His
spirit.

My soul waits in God

Psalms 62:5

For God alone my soul waits in silence and quietly submits to Him, For my hope is from Him

---

I *extend* joy

Galatians 5:22-23

But the fruits of the Spirit is love, joy, peace, patience, kindness, goodness, fruitfulness, gentleness, self-control. Against such things there is no law.

God will *establish* me and guard me *against* the evil one

---

2 Thessalonians 3:3

But the Lord is faithful, and He will strengthen you and will protect and guard you from the evil one.

I have a future filled with hope

Jeremiah 29:11

For I know the plans
and thoughts that I
have for you' says the
LORD,'plans for peace
and well-being and not
for disaster to give you
a future and a hope.

Assured by Abba

I will think good things because I become what I think

134

Proverbs 23:7

For as he thinks in his heart, so is he...

—————————

Greater is he that is in me than he that is in the world

—————————

1 John 4:4

Little children, you
are of God and you
belong to Him and
have overcome them;
because He who is in
you is greater than
he who is in the world.

God loves me unconditionally

---

1 John 3:1

See what an incredible quality of love the Father has shown to us, that we would be named and called and counted the children of God! And so we are! For this reason the world does not know us, because it did not know Him.

I extend peace

Galatians 5:22-23

But the fruits of the Spirit is love, joy, peace, patience, kindness, goodness, fruitfulness, gentleness, self-control. Against such things there is no law.

I can do all things through christ who strengthens me

Philippians 4:13

I can do all things
through Him who
strengthens and
empowers me

———————

God is with me wherever I go

———————

Joshua 1:9

"Have I not commanded you? Be strong and courageous! Do not be terrified or dismayed, for the LORD your God is with you wherever you go."

I hear the voice of God because I am his sheep

John 10:27

"The sheep that are My own hear My voice and listen to Me; I know them, and they follow Me.

The Lord is my rock and my fortress and my deliverer

Psalms 18:2

The Lord is my rock, my fortress, and the One who rescues me; My God, my rock and strength in whom I trust and take refuge...

I can come to God and ask for wisdom and he will guide me

James 1:5

If any of you lacks wisdom, he is to ask of God, who gives to everyone generously and without rebuke or blame, and it will be given to him.

I *extend* kindness

Galatians 5:22-23

But the fruits of the Spirit is love, joy, peace, patience, kindness, goodness, fruitfulness, gentleness, self-control. Against such things there is no law.

The lord hears me and answers me when I call him

Matthew 7:7

"Ask and keep on asking and it will be given to you; seek and keep on seeking and you will find; knock and keep on knocking and the door will be opened for you".

God's love
endures
forever

Psalms 136:1

Give thanks to the
Lord, for He is good;
For His lovingkindness
endure forever.

I was created with divine purpose

Genesis 1:27

So God created man in His own image, in the image and likeness of God He created him; male and female He created them.

I standout everywhere I go

Psalms 71:17

I am as a wonder to many, For You are my strong refuge.

I prevail over difficult situations and always come out victorious

---

Colossians 1:11

filled with the fruits of righteousness which comes through Jesus Christ, to the glory and praise of God.

I live by faith, not by sight

---

2 Corinthians 5:7

for we walk by faith, not by sight-

I extend goodness

Galatians 5:22-23

But the fruits of the Spirit is love, joy, peace, patience, kindness, goodness, fruitfulness, gentleness, self-control. Against such things there is no law.

The Lord will grant the desires of my heart

Psalms 37:4

Delight yourself in the Lord, And He will give you the desires and petitions of your heart.

I declare my body
is healed of all
things in Jesus
name

Isaiah 53:5

But He was wounded for our transgressions, He was crushed for our wickedness; The punishment for our wellbeing fell on Him, And by His stripes we are healed.

I will leave a financial legacy

Proverbs 13:22

A good man leaves an inheritance to his children's children, And wealth of the sinner is stored up for the righteous

---

I will diversify my income, investments, and skills in order to become wealthy

---

Ecclesiastes 11:2

Give a portion to seven, or even to eight, for you do not know what misfortune may occur on the earth.

I declare that this day, I have the mind of Christ

Philippians 2:5

Have this same attitude in yourselves which was in Christ Jesus,

I submit to The Lord

Psalms 62:5

For God alone my soul waits in silence and quietly submits to Him, For my hope is from Him

---

I extend faithfulness

Galatians 5:22-23

But the fruits of the Spirit is love, joy, peace, patience, kindness, goodness, fruitfulness, gentleness, self-control. Against such things there is no law.

Even before God made the world, he loved me

Ephesians 1:4

just as He chose us in Christ before the foundation of the world, so that we would be holy and blameless in His sight. In love

---

I will be content
in all things

Philippians 4:12

...In any and every circumstance I have learned the secret, whether well-fed or going hungry, whether having an abundance or being in need.

What the Lord started in my life, he will finish it

Phillippians 1:6

I am convinced and confident of this very thing, that He who has begun a good work in you will perfect and complete it until the day of Christ Jesus.

My bank account grows everyday so I will avoid debt

Proverbs 13:22

A good man leaves an inheritance to his children's children, and wealth of the sinner is stored up for the righteous

---

I *see* the beauty in *everything*

Ecclesiastes 3:11

He has made
everything beautiful
and appropriate in its
time. He has also
planted eternity in the
human heart- yet man
can not find out what
God has done from
the beginning to the
end.

God will keep me in perfect peace

Isaiah 26:3

You will keep in perfect and constant peace the one whose mind is steadfast, Because he trusts and takes refuge in You.

———————

I extend gentleness

———————

Galatians 5:22-23

But the fruits of the Spirit is love, joy, peace, patience, kindness, goodness, fruitfulness, gentleness, self-control. Against such things there is no law.

God's grace is sufficient for me

---

2 Corinthians 12:9

but He has said to me, "My grace is sufficient for you; for power is being perfected in weakness." Therefore, I will all the more gladly boast in my weaknesses, so that the power of Christ may dwell in me.

_____

God will supply all of my needs

_____

Philippians 4:19

And my God will liberally supply your every need according to His riches in glory in Christ Jesus.

The Lord is my refuge and strong tower

Psalms 61:3

For You have been a shelter and a refuge for me, A strong tower against the enemy.

Assured by Abba

_____

My past does not define me

_____

Isaiah 43:18-19

Do not remember the former things, Or ponder the things of the past. "Listen carefully, I am about to do a new thing...

Jesus cares for me

1 Peter 5:7

casting all your cares
on Him, for He cares
about you.

If God is for me, who can be against me

Romans 8:31

What then shall we say to all these things? If God is for us, who can be against us?

_____

My God is faithful

_____

2 Thessalonians 3:3

But the Lord is faithful, and He will strengthen you and will protect and guard you from the evil one.

I have self control

Galatians 5:22-23

But the fruits of the Spirit is love, joy, peace, patience, kindness, goodness, fruitfulness, gentleness, self-control. Against such things there is no law.

———————

I will call upon the Lord and pray to Him and He will hear me

———————

Jeremiah 29:12

Then you will call on Me and you will come and pray to Me, and I will hear and I will listen to you.

God goes before
me, he is with me,
and he will not
leave me or
forsake me

Deuteronomy 31:8

"It is the Lord who goes before you; He will be with you. He will not fail you or abandon you. Do not fear or be dismayed."

God's eyes are upon me and his ears are open to my prayers

---

1 Peter 3:12

FOR THE EYES OF THE LORD ARE UPON THE RIGHTOUS AND HIS EARS ARE ATTENTIVE TO THEIR PRAYER,...

God set me apart
by design, I wasn't
meant to look or
be like anyone

Deuteronomy 14:2

for you are set apart to the Lord your God; and the Lord has chosen you out of all the people who are on the earth to be a person for His own possession

---

I am a child of
the most high
God!

John 1:12

But to as many as did receive and welcome Him, He gave the right to become children of God, that is, to those who believe in His name-

About the Author

Samaja M. Stevenson was raised in the DFW area, where she currently resides. She loves the Lord and is passionate about bringing her generation closer to God.

Check out her previous work, How to Elevate Your Prayers: Volume 1. Available at www.shesfavorednetwork.com

To connect or for bookings, Contact Samaja at:
Socials: samstvnsn
Email: sammonaemgmnt@gmail.com
Ministry Email: renewmintx@gmail.com